Waiting for the Rain

Written by Katherine Goode • Illustrated by Tom Sladden

We waited for the rain,
but the rain never came.
Day after day,
we looked in the sky for clouds.
Day after day,
we waited for the cool winds to blow.
But every day,
it just got hotter and drier.

2

The wheat in the fields dried up
and turned to dust.
The water for the dam dried up
and turned to mud.
Even the flowers in Mom's garden dried up
under the hot, hot sun.
And every day,
it got hotter and drier.

6

The sheep in the fields
had to be fed by hand.
The water for the dam
had to be pumped by hand.
Even the flowers in Mom's garden
had to be watered by hand.
And every day,
it got hotter and drier.

At night, we lay awake
and listened for the rain.
We heard the cows
mooing in the fields.
We heard the crickets
singing in the grass.
We heard the wind
blowing in the trees.
But we didn't hear
the sound of rain.

The wind blew harder and harder.
It blew the roof off the barn.
It blew the branches off the trees.
It blew the topsoil from the fields.

Everything was covered with dust.

Then, suddenly, it was still.
The wind stopped blowing.
Everything was very still.

Then we heard the sound of the rain!

We raced outside
and danced in the rain.
The dam filled up,
and the ducks went for a swim.
The rain fell on the sheep
and washed them clean.
Even Mom's flowers perked up!

12

We splashed in the puddles
and got covered with mud.
We got mud on our arms
and mud on our hands.
We got mud on our legs
and mud on our toes.
We got mud on our hair
and on our noses and on our ears.
We were the muddiest
and happiest family around!